HOW TO RECOGNIZE GOD'S CHOSEN

HOW TO RECOGNIZE GOD'S CHOSEN

by
Jeremy Paden

Accents Publishing • Lexington, Kentucky • 2025

Printed in the United States of America

Accents Publishing
Editor: Katerina Stoykova
Cover Image by Christine Kuhn

Library of Congress Control Number: 2025943593
ISBN: 978-1-961127-18-0
First Edition

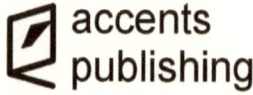

Accents Publishing is an independent press for brilliant voices. For a catalog of current and upcoming titles, please visit us on the Web at

www.accents-publishing.com

CONTENTS

for dani & lara
for evan & garrett

Why this going back and forth in my farness and exile?
— Mansur Al-Hallaj

God is at home; we are in the far country.
—*Holy the Firm*
Annie Dillard

PROLOGUE/
THE SPACE WHERE THE HEART SHOULD BE

for Christine Kuhn

take the space where the brain
should be & the space where
the heart should be & the space
where the bowels go, shuffle
them about like a conman
in a street corner shell game

place the bowels in the skull
& the heart in the stomach
shuffle them & shuffle them
all again until none can tell
bosom from head, belly
from heart, brain from bowels

I.

try pounding & when pounding fails, cut against the grain

some will swear the secret is to forget the heart in a bath of vinegar & salt until the hard connective tissues are eaten away. some will tell you slaughter the young as young as possible, that heart meat, like grass, is tender & sweet when just a shoot. some will insist on the use of cloisters & penitence, on the need to give one's backside to the world

but I say, we have been too long in a land of traffick, too long in a city of merchants, for too long have our hearts been sold to & bought by the lowest bidder. & our hearts are old & bitter. they are tired & have grown large & tough with age. no, there will be no tenderness until, bruised & battered. until the heart, like a seed, like a cedar shoot, is taken to the mountain high & planted

so climb the steps, take the flint blade in your hand, crack the chest & pound the heart, pound & mince & grind it down

I am done, said zhe, old & spent. so heart in hand & bleeding, I give it to you. give me nothing in return. I've worked it over & still it's tough. beat it & when your mallet has done what it can, slow braise it, then place it under your knife, cut against the grain, & scatter it to the winds

II.

who is this zhe
who speaks of sacrifice

whose heart is to be cut out
& pounded, to be served up
to the fire & the blade

who is this zhe
& who are those who follow

III.

zhe is the beloved

& hir life, like all lives,
is first blueprint, sketch

& then departure
        improvisation
yes, even deviance

legends swear otherwise, tell
of a child so self-possessed

so obedient to the plan
that jackals & cherry trees

asps & wandering tricksters
look on in wonder

tell of portents such that kings
covetous will slaughter
        even suckling babes

yet zhe is the beloved
& like all beloveds

zhe wonders, zhe doubts
zhe wanders, for no life
not even the beloved's
        is simple

IV.

scholars comb the archive
like a parent combs louse-ridden hair

diggers descend through layers
of detritus & ruin for the slightest residue

archivists & paleographers
read script like hunters do the tracks of prey

priests protect their mysteries
some by lording over the secrets

some by giving them away
like water, like air, like butterflies

the congregation debates the merits
grasps on to flotsam & jetsam

teachers argue over prepositions
& the drift of language over time

& the faithful disown each other
over the betrayal of translation

V.

a teaching

—after the 5th section of the Katha Upanishad

i.

the body is a house, a city even
a city with eleven gates
that breathes & grieves

a city born of mountain
            & of sacrifice
that gathers all unto itself
yes, even the accused
            even the slayer

ii.

the body is a city, a mountain
whose rivers & streams
are watered by rain & snow

& the mountain is the house
made glad by the song
            of snowmelt

iii.

the body is a house, the world even
a forest with its understory & overstory
with its broad sky above hills
& hills that smooth into plains

the body is a world where rivers
grow wide & slow at the mouth
where storks dance in the braids
of the delta & osprey dive
into shallow lagoons

the world is a city that is a mountain
that is a river that is a house that is a body
that gathers all life into its walls

VI.

zhe is numbered among the abandoned, bereft
counted among the newborns left to the elements
forgotten at the cliff's edge
                              but zhe will return

return to stand at the threshold & call all
the dispossessed to gather, all those turned out
given up, & they will come
                              come for a feast

a feast of stones & flowers, each will bring
what they have: the river-rounded quartz & the cold-
cracked flint, the violet & the dandelion

& they will bring their nests of straw & feather-down
knocked loose by the wind
                              no journalist, no professor
of political science, no writer of policy or film-script

will notice zhe or those gathered below the cliff
around the fire
                   but they will thrive, thrive on their flowers
& stones, they will live & thrive & turn to dust

zhe & all the congregation of god's chosen

VII.

an early story found in clay pots, scholars dispute whether zhe is a name, a pronoun, or an article

those in the congregation of the chosen who call themselves the faithful came to zhe & asked: how can we tell others what you are like, master

& zhe answered: no one is your master, certainly not I

to which one of them replied: but who will marshal us when we storm the temple?

& another: who will perch in the turret of the lead tank when we ride into Babylon?

& another still: who will write the new laws?

to which zhe answered: here is a well & here a bucket; let us draw water & drink while we still can. in time, the snows will all melt away, & this well will not be deep enough. but for now, we are together & we thirst, so let us drink

VIII.

zhe speaks not with knotted ropes
salves of spit, mud & herbs bruised

not with sound of thunder or clap of black
powders bright before dazzled eyes

whether zhe wields a sword, strings a bow
dons maille shirts to go down & enter the fight

accounts differ, who or when, what or how
god's chosen are & come, none can say

some swear zhe drinks of spirits with thirst
unquenched & dances with all the damned

some curse the name of those who think
zhe does not deny all pleasures of the flesh

yet when zhe tabernacles with us & shares
in the bitter cup of wine that all are given

none will know until after the pistol-whipped body
is taken down from the barbed wire fence

until after the body chained to the bumper of a truck
is dragged through city streets & left at the morgue

with no one to claim the corpse, with no one
to cry out:
        here, here lies the very goodness of god

IX.

a song of praise found among the earliest of manuscripts

zhe is in the hearth fire
in the hearth fire & in the well

zhe is in the water drawn up from the well
& in the water boiling in the kettle

zhe is the house with a hearth & a kettle
& is also the house guest

zhe is the host
& the knife

the knife that cuts the bread
& that also spreads the butter & the jam

zhe is the sour that leavens the dough
& the fire that cooks the bread

zhe is the fire & the bread
the host & the guest

the house & the water
& the knife

X.

throngs will come, throngs will press in on every side
at times this will seem like a mad frenzy, like the crush
of an angry mob
                    at times this will seem like the crazed
adoration of youth caught up in the throb of hearts
& hips & the rhythmic slapping of strings electrified
of heads lost to the pulse
                                at times this will seem like the faithful
going down to the river to bathe

but come they will
                    for who has seen such beauty
the beauty of the pure in heart, of the chosen
of a body that spins & dips
                                that catwalks & floorworks
through this crowded world, for no other reason
than there are times when life makes the body sing

this verily is that
                    zhe will stand on the shores of a lake
at sunset, will sit on the crest of a hill at noon
will pull away in the night to a mountain orchard
to be
        & the stillness of hir body will be heard
as a song, as a chant, a silbo gomero, a kulning

XI.

a pericope on belonging found in jars in a cave beside the cave scholars say was the first cave in which stories of zhe were found

among the gathered by the road zhe stood & preached a sermon made of questions:

does all cast seed that lands on the road get eaten by birds? might not some hitch a ride on soles, in the cuff of pants, or the tuft of fur that clumps around the fetlock? might not some find purchase in rich soil far from the sower's field?

& is the seed that lands among the rocks all destined to quick growth & sudden death from parching? might some not find a way to send roots to the ditch or to the edge of the field prepared with manure & wood ash?

what if we are seed, not soil?

what if we were judged not by our fruit ripening in the sun but by our roots, how they sought out water & loam? how they worked with the roots of other plants to give back to the earth minerals harvested from the sky? by our stalk & leaves, how they grew toward the sun, regardless of whether their growth was narrow & straight?

what if what mattered was only that we grew where our roots found a place to thrive?

XII.

zhe is the beloved

the beloved is the homeless boy
who's wandered down from a country
                    named Great River

who's tricked nights in the berths
of tractor trailers for southbound rides
for rides away, away, away

who sits on the curb in a cul-de-sac
hir does not know & says:
                    I wanted

to bed down alone in the woods,
but that's not how the highway spins

XIII.

zhe will know chosenness not
in the rain that does or does not fall
not in the hive heavy with honey
or dry & silent after collapse
but in the questions asked

will know chosenness not
in the light or darkness shed
by any answer to any question asked
but in the asking of the questions

will know chosenness not
in the wet, golden light of chosenness
but in the questions dry & dark

will know chosenness not
but in the no & the but & the what of the ask

zhe will know chosenness not

XIV.

the faithful sniff about
for evidence of being chosen

the faithful divide & divide
again until division stands
as the only proof of their fidelity

this is not that
                some faithful proclaim
& they pare the stories down
with pumice stones & scissors

all those repetitions
all the bothersome differences
in all those repetitions

smoothed over, cut out
so the dead can bury the living

& a third school
                & a fourth
arise & preach

winnowing forks & wind
& little else

this is a test
        they preach
god tests all those
who are chosen

XV.

a late story found in a cave that some believe to be the library of a loose collection of desert hermits

once when zhe had left the crowds flowing into & out of basement lounges & speakeasies to find a quiet spot, once zhe had climbed all 102 stories to the top deck, zhe found hir was not alone, not even there, high above the city, yes, even there, people, people with questions:

tell us, they said, when one falls asleep in matins, should we pinch the slumberer awake so they take up their prayers again in earnest

to which zhe responded: let them sleep, please, let them sleep, give them your lap for a pillow & let them sleep

XVI.

the beloved's body wants love
    like an ache, like a hole in the gums
    which the tongue probes & prods
       & it wants not love

wants touch & is sick of touch
sick of the smell of hands & thighs
of hair & nails, of flaking skin

the beloved's body prances about
    to be seen:
      o what abandon
      proud as a corpse flower

& at times is that armored lizard
    that bites its own tail & curls up
    into a crown of thorns

XVII.

who is this zhe
& who are
those who follow

XVIII.

  a praise song

zhe is a whale that dives
dives into twilight waters
& dreams hir is a hummingbird
that flits from flower to flower
from perch to perch
as it truths out nectar

zhe is a hummingbird
that dreams hir is a jesus bug
that skims across the surface
of streams & ponds
in & out of sun & shadow

zhe is a jesus bug
that dreams hir is a giant squid
that slips through the fissures
of the deep like a wraith
like a hawk on the wing
that rides the winds

zhe is a hawk that's a giant squid
that dreams hir is a butterfly
that dreams hir is a whale that dives
into twilight waters that dreams
hir is a jesus bug that is a hummingbird

XIX.

the gathered split into the faithful
on one side & the faithful on the other,
you are not the faithful, the faithful say,

we have seen you wash your left hand
before your right, have seen you eat of foods
forbidden on days of new moon & old

harlot & heretic, welfare queen & drag
are flung from soapboxes on street corners
as the faithful thunder, these are the latter days

of false prophets, woe to you, the faithful say
to the faithful in tent meetings, you who return
home late on days of solstice & equinox

surely these are the end times, days of holocaust
& dragons, woe to the belly dancers & carnivalists,
we are the remnant, the chosen, the set apart

from the first for life beside the crystal lake,
for the watchtower set among the stars,
these are the hard days of ascent & purge,

see how orderly we keep our lawns, our dress
how we stand at the door of our abundance
& toss out wisdom like candy,

see how we slam shut the high, holy doors
of communion & jubilee & toss the stale bread
& fish tails of our sated congregation to the pigs

XX.

zhe is a seeker who seeks not as a bee
that flits from flower to flower

but as a whale that dives deep
                              deep beyond
the realms of sunlight

zhe is a seeker that knows to search the depths
is folly, a shameless tempting of god

but zhe is a seeker whose search looks
like a leap into nothingness

looks a fall
                    from great heights

XXI.

zhe is the beloved

the beloved is the minister's daughter
who died to hirself

who buried the name they chose for hir
& after this death rose again

zhe is the minister's son gone down
to the river to be baptized with a new name

the name zhe says was
        always hir true name

XXII.

zhe is the beloved
yet zhe will know chosenness not

even though zhe, as both mirror
& sun, shines bright as morning
bright as one whose feet are brass

even though zhe, as both star & moon,
is bright as burnished obsidian
bright as the water at the bottom of a well

still zhe will know not if the light
shines out or bounces off

XXIII.

a teaching found in the desert library

    —*after the* Tao Te Ching *&* Emily Dickinson

in the city square under the arch, or perhaps under the bridge, zhe stands & says:

pain is empty & use will not drain it. it has that element of blank that covers the abyss with trance. it is deep & runs below in caverns & courses through all of life. it is the ancestor. out of it rise myriad beings, yet pain claims no authority, makes no demands, asks only not to be thought on or worried after. face it & you will not see it; sneak up behind it & it has no haunches. it is the fording of a river, swift & swollen with midwinter ice. it is an uncarved block in the valley that does not give up its name

XXIV.

zhe is the beloved

the beloved is the neighbor
who no longer remembers
why or when they took to drink

whose intemperate days
slide into nights bitter & slip
into mornings of gall & bile

& the beloved is the neighbor's
fleeing partner polished down
to hard sadness & bright anger

stripped to nothing but the scent
of vinegar & acid that clings
to the bedsheets & the breath

XXV.

zhe will wake one morning or evening
it matters not, will rise one late afternoon
in the middle of a meal of stewed fava beans

& flat bread, or at its end, for the earth
will have rattled, walls crumbled, it matters not
if from missile strikes or winds & waves or moving plates

roofs will have turned to rubble, floors
to dust & nothingness, terror & numbness
will visit together, for the world

will have looked zhe full in the face or maybe
in the back of the head as zhe flees or stays behind
to build again a life among the ruins

the world will have looked at zhe
& said: you, your name is scapegoat
                                    exile

XXVI.

zhe is the beloved

the beloved swims the river
with hir child on hir back

& when the current is too strong
with hir child on hir stomach & chest

& the beloved is the child shivering
& the beloved is the child gasping for breath

XXVII.

zhe will smell of ashes
& oranges, of origin & anise .

will call out to stone & mud
as brother, to wind & air as sister

& will wait for father tree
& mother river to answer

tree & stone, mud & wind
river & air will speak

when they speak & none
will know the difference

not even zhe, between
their visitation & silence

XXVIII.

sometimes god's chosen decides, no longer
do I want to be god's chosen, sometimes
zhe walks out on it all & asks: god,
who are you to choose whose are yours

sometimes zhe goes & sits under a willow,
beside a stream & says: no, my body
is temple to nothing & no one
& says: my body is stone, nothing else

& asks: what is soul to stone & what
is stone but earth baked hard & dry,
to which god, a hungry axolotl, says:

fine, you are soulless stone
& still my chosen gastrolith

XXIX.

the faithful will ask themselves
   how can zhe be

both tiger & swan
    sun & moon
  stone & river

& also cloud
   pushed by the wind—

the breath that trembles
   the leaves & ripples the water

is slight & unpredictable

   too mutable—

this is all too much
    a patchwork
     quilt

& we need a hero story
    in three easy movements

XXX.

according what zhe receives, zhe speaks
at the intersection, at the market, in the middle
of traffic, parched tongue in hand zhe waits

for the word to descend, for the wave
of god's visitation to rush into the dry estuary
of the mouth like a tidal bore

& knows once the waves of joy & dread settle
& the word has come & gone
                                        loneliness
& wailing is all that's left

even when the word is love
even when the word is peace
or mercy or grace

XXXI.

a pericope found on parchment, stitched to the back pages of the earliest incunabula

—*after Julian of Norwich's* Revelations of Divine Love

give us a teaching on love, the gathered once asked, is it true that lovers will never fall or falter, that the beloved will always keep them bound & protected, that they will always know they are loved & never wander?

& zhe responded: this was never shown me, instead it was shown that love will hold them, hold them as they leave & they return, as they fall & get up, even as they fall & keep falling, even as they believe they are not loved

XXXII.

zhe is the beloved

the beloved is the mother
who has fled the war with her children
with her children & with her injured
                              husband in tow

fear & weariness pool in the beloved's eyes
they say: god, we are here & can't go back
here & all the words we've hoarded are useless

& though zhe has no words
zhe does not need them to say:

loneliness & worry
       worry & fear

fear & homesickness
       homesickness & exile

XXXIII.

zhe will wake to bird song at dawn & to wet gardenia
on bright breeze & call this new country paradise

zhe will say: yes, this is paradise, & will gawk
its streets of crystal buildings until the beggars

& zhe will know this country pleasants a secret dark
will think all the plenty is not abundance & saturdays

& all zhe had ignored when calling this land beulah
will come to mind, all the sirens & the weeping

but still the dawn & the songbird a lightness will bring
& zhe will call this new country not paradise

& zhe will say to this not paradise of wailing & sirens
of abundance of want & weeping beneath the crystal buildings

of plenty that is not blessing & of secrets darkly pleasanted
zhe will say: I am the dawn & the song

& zhe will rise full of gardenia & walk to the wailing
& sit with the sirens & saturday with those who bring death

saturday with them a lunch of june beulahs
of gardenia blessings wet with breeze

XXXIV.

a pericope in verse

—*with some lines by Walt Whitman*

zhe showed up at temple & read
from the scrolls, some accounts say
zhe was pushed to the town's edge

some accounts say when zhe read
the scrolls all that was difficult was at last
understood, some accounts say no one

noticed, because who does more than gasp
when gomer walks in & ascends the dais?
who does more than laugh when the prodigal

still dressed in rags & stench believes god
to have spoken more than words of condemnation?
but zhe walked in, head high & mouth full of song

song of self & celebration, of you & of love
electric, of me & of sunshine & motion of waves
o such songs, o such gleesome songs

XXXV.

yet another pericope

is not purity of heart simply to will one thing, the faithful asked, & is not unity of will to want only that which god wants? zhe, they said, your teachings make up our morning song, our midday prayer, our evening lullaby

to which zhe replied: have you studied how to get a ruler to give up their belt & signet ring? have you ever sat on a rock & beat back the vultures come to feast on the livers of those whom the state has called traitor? have you fled with your child in the night under the desert stars?

zhe, we have come to you for water, for that bread that does not turn to maggots by morning, for wine, we need wine to cross these angry seas. we did not ask for stories of concubines & harlots, for stories of the terrible fate of traitors. we are solving for heaven & the equation is hard

XXXVI.

a sermon by zhe in five points

—*after Juan Felipe Herrera*

1.   zhe once said: it's easy. walk up to the gates of the city of gratitude. walk in & through & you will have arrived

2.   when asked how do we get there, zhe responded: there is no map. no one to say, climb through fields of feathery red quinoa planted beside stone corrals, go up & over the side of the extinct volcano where pine & palm grow side by side & there in the old lakebed of the caldera, the city you seek

3.   zhe further said: some have breathed their way into stillness & arrived. some have driven their cars at breakneck speeds & crashed through the granite walls of the city & found themselves weepy with gratitude. some were born when the moon of thankfulness shone on the night-blooming cactus & have only ever known the joy of thank you. some were set apart for suffering

4.   & the gathered replied: zhe, this teaching is hard. & zhe answered: how you get there is how you get there. there will be days & months, years even, where you'll wander & the swamps that make the anaconda happy will be to you a hell. there will be those who try to sell you secret maps & potions mixed from roots & seeds no chemist has ever known. you'll grow short of breath & sore. all this is true

5.   & zhe added: you cannot study your way to gratitude. the guanaco that has escaped the puma & the puma that feasts on the huemul & the condor that tends to the remains are all residents & neighbors

6.   you were told this was a five-point sermon, zhe concluded, but five, six, the grateful don't care, the grateful have arrived

XXXVII.

zhe will see the bird in the sanctuary
that flew in through the window & died
beside the altar
                      broken from hunger & thirst
& will believe it a sacrifice & also
the snakes trampled by trucks on the road

zhe will smell the smoke of a million acres
burned & call it a holocaust pleasing & meet
before god

zhe will see the landfills
the dumpsters overflowing with discard
& the streets abandoned to decay

zhe will wade through the offal & refuse
collected in ponds beside the slaughter fields

                              & fall prostrate
fall prostrate & say:
                    this is a site holy & sanctified

for zhe is counted among god's chosen
& to the pure all things are pure

XXXVIII.

the faithful came to zhe
& demanded a song of zion,
so zhe turned & chanted:

    praise the sturgeon & the lungfish
    praise the ginkgoes & echidnas
    the puzzle monkey tree & the horseshoe crab

but zhe, the faithful said, we want
a song of heaven, of everlasting life,
so zhe turned again & sang:

    praise the resurrection plant & lichen
    the snapping turtle & the hellbender
    praise the yew, the bristlecone pine, & the sacred fig

but zhe, sing to us of a time outside time,
sing to us of the great beyond,
so zhe turned & lifted hir voice:

    praise the work of roots, of rhizomes & mycelium
    praise, praise the eastern juniper & the shaggy-maned moss
    the ant, praise the ant & bloodroot, trout lilies & wild ginger, praise

XXXIX.

zhe is the beloved
hir body is a continent wild
& populated
              with alien colonies
that harvest what they can
from gut & blood

colonies
         that tabernacle where
they find a toehold
& fight to thrive
          as best they can

before hir body
          like all bodies

fails

          in countless
                   intimate ways

XL.

a sermon in verse

the world is a house on fire
                    zhe said

& when zhe said house, zhe meant
cathedral, mosque, temple in the heart
of the city, gone up in flames, gone
down to ash

the world is a mosque on fire

& when zhe said world, zhe meant
body & when zhe said fire
zhe meant st mary baptist, meant 16th street
meant some row house on osage avenue

the world is a body on fire
                    zhe said

& when zhe said body, zhe meant
a gothic cathedral in the heart
of mosul, a temple on osage avenue
a house in the middle of jerusalem
a living church in a car on a street
in texas or michigan or georgia
a row house full of dancers
at the corner of south orange & esther

& when zhe said fire, zhe meant
arsonist, police, drones
meant a man with a gun

the world is a house & it's on fire
& when zhe said house, zhe meant body
& when zhe said body, zhe meant world
& when zhe said world, zhe meant holocaust

the world is a fire that smolders on the edge of town
fire is a dancehouse, an everlasting furnace
it's a body bright & fallen from heaven

the body is a house that is the world
                    that is the world in flames

XLI.

proud in themselves the faithful came to zhe
again & also in the temples they had built, proud,
& in the shine of sun through the thin alabaster
walls of their councils, proud, & proud in the logic

they had syllogized to raise up a labyrinth
of faith & they, proud in their robes & rituals,
came & said: did you not ask this of us
when you asked will there be mustard seeds

scattered & grown into trees to be cut down
then planed & hammered into temples? the door
stands open, ignore the gargoyles that keep

the cursed away, come, the table is spread for you
we've not lost heart, come, as we have come to you,
come in from the cold & dark, you are our guest

XLII.

zhe said: the world is god's body given for all

& the faithful responded: yes, this is why we have built these temples. this is why we have taken the children of the undeserving to train them up, to inscribe this truth into their very flesh

zhe said: their body is my body

the faithful, in turn, replied: this is why we have sent them to boarding schools to faith them in the language of our truth

& all the while, zhe stood on the back porch, hungry

XLIII.

at the height of fig season
& pleased with themselves
the faithful came & said:
our orchard is your orchard

zhe gazed upon their barren plot
& they said: we have followed
all the teachings you gave us—
hands have been severed

eyes gouged out, we have cursed
the trees & we've left the dead
to bury themselves, we are

the faithful who hate father
& mother, who've sold all to buy
extra lamp oil & these guns

XLIV.

the faithful came to zhe & said: we have heard some teach that doubt should be doubted, that to ask & seek & not to be certain is to be but a plastic bag in the bed of a pickup truck, lifted out & tossed about by the contradicting winds cast off by eighteen-wheelers racing to deliver their goods

& zhe answered: yes, the certain are so very much like tractor trailers barreling down a mountain speedway

unhappy, the faithful responded: tell us about doubt & what we should do with those among us who doubt, for doubt is an acid that eats metal, a virus that can be caught unawares

& zhe answered: I give unto you that which was given to me, mercy, mercy is greater than doubt

XLV.

a song of disputed provenance about which some scholars argue that each I am statement should read zhe is

I am the remnant
the remnant is a tent peg
left out in the rain & sun
that holds the cloth taut
that watches the stars
& the moon & is sniffed
& pissed on by jackals

I am the garden plot
clear cut & mismanaged
the garden plot
& also the blighted chestnut
that still sends up shoots
from the roots before
the blight latches on

I am the city burned
city turned to ash & salt

I am the stone
the stone by the wayside
that no one sees
stone that could be
a pillow for dreams
or a fountain of water
stone that is a pebble
a pebble in the shoe

I am the remnant
the remnant is a stump
a worn-out queen
in the rotten hollow
of a tree full of sour honey

fussing over hir dress & face
ready to descend the staircase
into the arms of hir jailers

XLVI.

zhe drinks from a cup
poured out
      by others

this seems like entrapment
like a blessing that is also a curse

a simple meal of roasted boar
or truffles & yam
served before the final

undoing

XLVII.

another teaching in verse
—*after Kakuzo Okakura's* The Book of Tea

the body is a hut
woven of grasses
out on the prairie
under the open sky

a lodge thatched
from long-stemmed
turfgrass & twigs

it smells of beeswax
acorn & tobacco

smells of the earth
to which it returns

XLVIII.

zhe will not have prepared for death
                              or its aftermath
no lines of succession, no contingency plans

zhe will have heard the heralds, seen the signs
the mob assembled at the jail on horseback
                                        with torches

this lapse, this denial that all things end
                                    even one's own life
is not the delusion of those convinced
they are destined for greatness

foreboding has always been with hir
like a shadow lengthening

the choice not to name dusk dusk
                              comes not
from a hope against the fall of night

the choice not to name dusk dusk comes
from the knowledge that still a light shines
& while there is light there is work

so zhe visits the congregation gathered by the fires
& watches them bow & rise, rise & bow

& zhe smiles & turns to leave & then the bullet
to right side of the face
                          the shotgun, revolver
knife pulled from a coat
                          straight to the chest
to the neck

after which zhe will say to death:
                          welcome, welcome

XLIX.

zhe is the beloved

the beloved's body hangs, tangled
in a barbed-wire fence

              the beloved's
body runs through the streets
lies twitching by the bed, lies crumpled
on the porch

          the beloved's body sleeps
under the bridge, beside the bridge, behind
the fence in a tent city

          the beloved's body
lies chained behind a truck, stripped naked
beside a dumpster

          the beloved's body stumbles
back to bed
      stumbles back to hir holding cell

L.

zhe is now an allegory
abecedarians recount hir life
k is for hir kindness & golden kumquats
t is for the tree of virtues

rose windows of stained glass
show zhe with a lamb in arms
dove in hand, asp trampled underfoot

in comic books & calendars
zhe dances with lotus in a river
lounges with lions & swans
in a colony of lepers

children learn of the dream cities
zhe built in the clouds, grandmothers
send zhe's ethics on greeting cards

this much is known, zhe was an I
for whom dogs, mules, stiff-necked
or docile, were also equally an I

LI.

books will be burned
                    defenestrated
like burgomasters
then set aflame in the plaza

mobs will throng
                    & blaze
in righteousness

these are not the teachings
of zhe
            they will shout

            who has the time
for these hard lessons
                    in meekness

we have come for king
not a fool

& the faithful will bar
the door
            to the library

& scrape & scalpel out
the words
            they do not like

& the faithful will work
through long cold nights
until their god looks
just like them

LII.

the congregation of god's chosen
will find zhe on the mountain
flower in hand

some will say it was a bud
a cherry yet to bloom

others a field lily, a lotus
some a tulip, tall & bright

some will call the flower sermon
call it love, call it death

& they will turn from hir
to speak its message

& will say, we all are flowers picked
& bundled into a bouquet of sand verbena
& primrose, of paintbrush & prairie sage

some will say, no, only zhe is
a flower, a golden daffodil

others will argue the flower is but chaff
to be burned, they will call this all idolatry
for no created thing, neither in heaven
nor on earth is divine

& when the gathered turn back to hir
to say, teach us the lesson of the flower

to ask, finally, is it prayer, is it gift
is it life, are we, too, flowers

they will turn & find only a goatsbeard
big & white & gone to seed

A NOTE OF GRATITUDE

This collection was started in 2016, during the June Lexington Poetry Month. And so, I first want to thank that community of writers. All of them: Hap Houlihan, for dreaming up the idea; Christopher McCurry and Bronson O'Quinn, for keeping it going; Kate Fadick, Pauletta Hansel, Karen George, Liz Prather, Nettie Farris, Denis Preston, H. B. Elam, and so many more who commented on those first drafts; and, of course, the community of writers here in Lexington that have been a part of my life: Tina Andry, Sean Corbin, Kate Hadfield, Jay McCoy, Bianca Spriggs, Eric Scott Sutherland, Katerina Stoykova, K. Nicole Wilson, John Lackey. I must also thank those who have, over the years, taken time to read and comment on the various drafts of these poems: Shauna Morgan, Martha Gehringer, Dave Harrity, Gerald Coleman, Zoe Strecker, and especially Carrie Green and Kristina Erny, you both know that without those days before, during, and after the pandemic during which we shared poems and life stories this book would not be. As always, I must thank the Affrilachian Poets for taking me in when I barely had a poem to my name. Where would any of us be without each other and this great town chock-a-block with writers and the small kindnesses we imperfectly show each other?

ACKNOWLEDGMENTS

The following poems have appeared in earlier versions here, sometimes under other numbers:

- "zhe will know chosenness not" appeared as "how to recognize god's chosen, ix," *The Messenger Is Sudden Thunder: Selections from LexPoMo June 2016*, Workhorse, 2017

- "try pounding & when pounding fails" appeared in *The Tenderness Project*, 2018.

- "throngs will come, throngs will press in on every side" appeared as "how to recognize god's chosen iii," *Taos Journal of International Poetry and Art*, Spring 2019

- "zhe will wake one morning or evening" appeared as "how to recognize god's chosen vii," *Taos Journal of International Poetry and Art*, Spring 2019

- "the congregation of god's chosen will find" appeared as "how to recognize god's chosen xx," *Taos Journal of International Poetry and Art*, Spring 2019

- "the faithful came to zhe & demanded a song of zion" appeared as "how to recognize god's chosen, xxxviii," *Appalachian Review*, Winter 2022

- "zhe will see the bird in the sanctuary" appeared as "how to recognize god's chosen, xxxii," *About Place Journal*, vol. 7, issue 2, Dec. 2022

- "a sermon in five points" appeared as "how to recognize god's chosen, xxxiii," *About Place Journal*, vol. 7, issue 2, Dec. 2022

- "a sermon in verse / the world is a house on fire" appeared as "how to recognize god's chosen, xxxiv," *About Place Journal*, vol. 7, issue 2, Dec. 2022

- "a teaching / give us a teaching on love" appeared as "how to recognize god's chosen, xxvi," *Cincinnati Review*, miCRo, March 2024

- "the faithful came to zhe & said, we have heard some teach that doubt" appeared as "how to recognize god's chosen, xxxix," *Cincinnati Review*, miCRo, March 2024

- "a teaching / the body is a house, a city even," appeared as "how to recognize god's chosen, v," *The Louisville Review*. Louisville: Fleur de Lis Press, vol. 96

- "a teaching found in the desert library / in the city square under the arch," appeared as "how to recognize god's chosen, xxiii," *The Louisville Review*. Louisville: Fleur de Lis Press, vol. 96

- "at the height of fig season," appeared as "how to recognize god's chosen, xliii," *The Louisville Review*. Louisville: Fleur de Lis Press, vol. 96

ABOUT THE AUTHOR

Jeremy Paden was born in Milan, Italy (1974) and is professor of Latin American literature at Transylvania University in Lexington, Kentucky and on faculty at Spalding University's low-residency MFA. He is also a poet and a translator. He is the author of multiple chapbooks and full-length collections of poems in both English and Spanish. His first book of poems, *Broken Tulips*, was a chapbook published by Accents Publishing in 2013. These are: *ruina montium* (Broadstone Books, 2016), *prison recipes* (Broadside Books, 2018), *ruina montium* (Valparaíso ediciones, 2018), *world as sacred burning heart* (3: A Taos Press, 2021), *Un poema rápido en vez de un himno* (Santa Rabia Poetry, 2024), *Imágenes del mundo flotante* (Alcorce Ediciones, 2024). Also, his bilingual *Self-Portrait as an Iguana* (Valparaíso USA, 2021) was named co-winner of the inaugural Poeta en Nueva York Prize. And, his bilingual and illustrated children's book *Under the Ocelot Sun / Bajo el sol del ocelote* (Shadelandhouse Modern Press, 2020), on the migrant caravan crisis, won a 2020 Campoy-Ada Prize awarded by the North American Academy of the Spanish Language for Children's Literature in Spanish. As a translator, he has published translations of contemporary Argentine, Bolivian, Chilean, Colombian, Mexican, Panamanian, Peruvian, Spanish, and Uruguayan poetry. His Spanish language translation of Ada Limón's *The Hurting Kind* has recently been published in Spain with Valparaíso Ediciones.

www.ingramcontent.com/pod-product-compliance
Lightning Source LLC
Chambersburg PA
CBHW031253120626
46545CB00007B/2800